# MINDSHIFT

*If you change your
mind, you change your
life. 1 day at a time*

L I N D A   L E E

**author**HOUSE®

*AuthorHouse™*
*1663 Liberty Drive*
*Bloomington, IN 47403*
*www.authorhouse.com*
*Phone: 833-262-8899*

*Published by AuthorHouse  05/10/2022*

*ISBN: 978-1-6655-5963-8 (sc)*
*ISBN: 978-1-6655-5962-1 (e)*

*Print information available on the last page.*

*Scripture quotations marked NIV are taken from the Holy Bible, New International Version®. NIV®. Copyright © 1973, 1978, 1984 by International Bible Society. Used by permission of Zondervan. All rights reserved. [Biblica]*

*This book is printed on acid-free paper.*

*"Didn't we say to you in Egypt, 'Leave us alone; let us serve the Egyptians'? It would have been better for us to serve the Egyptians than to die in the desert!"*

*Moses answered the people, "Do not be afraid. Stand firm and you will see the deliverance the Lord will bring you today. The Egyptians you see today you will never see again. The Lord will fight for you; you need only to be still." Exodus 14:12–14*

Israel was not yet a week out of Egypt and they already distorted the past, thinking that it was better for them in Egypt than it really was. At this point, Moses had no idea how God would help them in this situation. All he knew was God certainly would help. In a sense, Moses knew he was in such a bad situation that God had to come through. Moses told the people of Israel to stop. This is often the Lord's direction to the believer in a time of crisis. Despair will cast you down, keeping you from standing. Fear will tell you to retreat. Impatience will tell you to do something now. Presumption will tell you to jump into the Red Sea before it is parted. Yet as God told Israel, He often tells us to simply stand still and hold our peace as He reveals His plan. Moses didn't know what God would do, but he knew God would come through on their behalf. He knew that God would save His people and that the enemies of the Lord would be destroyed. Moses could say to Israel, "The Lord will fight for you."

When we see that our only help is God, we are more likely to trust Him. Sometimes it is the little things (the things we think we can do in our own strength) that get us down, not the big things that we know only God can do. We sometime knowingly and unknowingly act as Israel acted due to misleading, false account or impression; that has been misrepresented by the circumstances of life, we choose to live in an uncomfortable situation because we are afraid of change. So many have chosen an abusive relationship and made themselves believe it was better than it really was.

So many have chosen unhappy lives because they have convinced themselves that their situation was better than it really is and causes them to live their lives unknowingly in bondage. Mindshift positions us to properly receive victory instead of accepting defeat. The Israelites mindset closely resembles the 21$^{st}$ century church, they are stuck in anesthetizing (deprive of feeling or awareness) conformity. In this state you are so busy trying to fit in you forget that God created you to stand out, he called you to be set apart. Mindshift is designed to cause the real you to wake up because you been bound, broke, and in a state of depravity for far too long. Many of you may feel like you have been in this place too long to change now, but if you would change your mind, you can change your life one day at a time.

**In the spaces below, answer the question**

**WHO AM I?**

_____

_____

_____

_____

_____

_____

_____

_____

_____

_____

Hey there, I know you are thinking wow, no introduction, warning or nothing, you open the book and then bam, there is work to be done. Yep, that's how life sometimes comes at us. One minute we are excited about something and then out of nowhere a change of plans.

The objective of this activity is to have a record of our reality before and after this journey.

Have you ever asked yourself these questions or had these thoughts?

- Why am I here?
- Why should I live?
- If I were dead nobody would miss me
- I have no one that I can really count on
- Tired of living but too afraid to die

Have you struggled or continue to struggle even now to understand your purpose in life?

Have you suffered in silence, helping others when you need help yourself?

Have you encouraged others when you needed encouragement yourself?

Have you ever contemplated suicide, but you push to live for the well-being of others?

Do you find yourself battling depression, and because you are so well at covering it up with a smile, no one knows, so you feel like no one cares?

And because of these feelings you feel alone and sometimes rejected.

If these questions or comments have triggered something in you that has caused you to feel anger, scared, or maybe even sad; if these questions have caused tears to fill your eyes, or you feel this overwhelming urge of shame, and you must protect the secret because no one can ever know; has your heart begun to beat a little faster and your breathing increased and just because you have read the words, you want to close the book because you feel exposed, and you do not like this feeling? **WAIT**! DO NOT STOP NOW!!

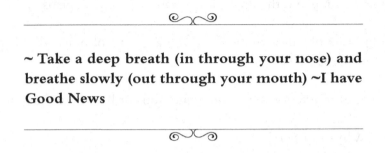

**~ Take a deep breath (in through your nose) and breathe slowly (out through your mouth) ~I have Good News**

YOU ARE NOT ALONE! Take a deep breath (in through your nose) and breathe slowly (out through your mouth), and say to yourself, I AM NOT ALONE.

Yes, you are not alone and there is a reason behind your madness. This manuscript is designed to force individuals into a position to explore why we do what we do. Throughout this journey we are going to be required to come face-to-face with some painful memories to identify the problems in our lives. We will then learn how to replace patterns, damaging habits, and attitudes. And lastly, we will develop ways to shift our way of thinking to develop new healthy habits and behaviors.

**Get your mirror, tissue, something to write with, a drink, and a snack.**

**Are you ready?**

**LET'S GO!!!**

**Let's talk about Beautiful Bondage**

When I was a child, I wanted to be older, but if I am honest, this mess is not what I imagined!

If we would take a few moments to think about the above phrase, it describes more people than we think. This saying does not have an age limit, income limit, nor does it have color boundaries. If we are honest, we all have had a moment when we felt overwhelmed because things seemed to be out of our control. But there are some of us that believe that this statement is our life. And until we work at readjusting our mindset and making healthy thinking habits a priority in our lives, we won't see much change in our life. Mind shifting is the art of arts. We should study our lives carefully and take the time to reflect. Asking ourselves the hard questions that could change our lives forever. Who am I? Why do I do what I do?

Oftentimes we condition our living to our upbringing, past mistakes, pain, betrayal or violations. For example, being reared in a place of poverty causes one to see life differently than one who has had everything they needed as a child. One bad decision can change the course of your future. Being molested or raped as a child can alter how we view day-to-day life. There is a place called "silenced" that many of us have entered and never left. Where is this place, how do I get there, and have I ever been there? The funny thing about this place is you never have to leave your home, because this place can be found in your mind and more times than not, you get there by no fault of your own. If you have had childhood trauma, chances are you have and may still be trapped in this dreadful place called "Silence."

Silence is a cause to become silent: prohibited or prevented from speaking. You may be saying, well, this does not include me because I can speak. In fact, I have been considered loud a time or two. The shift starts now. Silenced is not an inability to physically talk. Silenced is a state of being trapped in your mind and body. It feels like you are mentally in a closet and afraid to come out. Some describe it as having walls up to protect themselves. There is nothing wrong with having healthy boundaries, but when these boundaries are set due to unhealthy, hurtful situations, your experiences have silenced you. A negative experience has placed you in a mental closet that you peep out from but have never fully escaped. If we are honest, like the children of Israel we have adapted our lives to this place and never attempted to leave because we have become accustomed to this place and sadly, we think it is safe here. Leading us to live a life of mistaken identity, because we are now living from a place of hurt, devastation, fear, and brokenness. I call this a life of beautiful bondage. Now, think about your beautiful bondage, what it looks like, what it feels like, and how has it caused you to see the world around you. Congratulations! You have taken the first step!

Homework

What could your beautiful bondage be?

_____

_____

_____

_____

_____

_____

_____

_____

_____

_____

_____

_____

_____

_____

_____

_____

**The greatest tragedy in life is not death, but life without purpose.**

**-Dr. Myles Munroe-**

Let us begin by examining the words "Life" and "Purpose." The dictionary defines the word life as the existence of an individual human being or animal. It is the period between the birth and death of a living thing, especially a human being. The word purpose means the reason something was done or created or for which something exists. Both definitions have something in common, both purpose and life deal with the existence of a person. Why am I here? What is my reason for being here? Why do I exist? Why was I created? Until we have answers to these questions, we will not live a fulfilling, purpose-filled life. Instead, we will unknowingly misunderstand, misuse, abuse, and mishandle opportunities that have been placed before us. We will misinterpret things that are meant to bless us while accepting things that are meant to destroy us. Let's explore. Our first activity is designed to help us explore these questions: Who am I? Who do people say that I am? What do others see when they see me?

Because I have made the commitment to being with you this entire journey, I will do the activity first. Who am I? Who do people say that I am? What do others see when they see me?

**When I think of myself, the things that come to mind are these: I am a believer, I am a minister of the gospel of Jesus Christ, I am the wife of a very loving and caring God-fearing man. I am the mother of four beautiful girls. I like spending time with family, laughing, and having a good time. I have a passion for being a connecting point for the lost to hear and experience the grace and love of God and I think that's what people see when they see me. I also have a problem with saying "no."**

Now it's your turn, who are you, and what do people see when they see you, now that you can be two different things? Use the space below to write a brief description of yourself and who you think people expect you to be

_____

_____

_____

_____

_____

_____

_____

_____

_____

_____

_____

_____

_____

_____

_____

_____

_____

Great Job! We did it! Seem easy to write what we know to be true. Go ahead and celebrate today because the real work begins tomorrow.

Welcome back! Wait, is this how others really perceive us, or is this how we think or want others to perceive us? Because I am on a quest to find the truth. I sent out a group text to family and friends who I knew would be honest, and I asked these same questions. What do you see when you see me? Describe me in three words, and some of their responses were in line with what I felt. Their answers were "nice," "sweet," "smart," "woman of God," "motherly," "shy," "self-controlled," "caring," "talented," "considerate," "inspiring," "motivational," "giving heart" and "loving." Although all this sounded good and made me smile, I needed to go a little deeper because I am now seeking to be the best I can be. So, I sent a second text: "Thanks for such encouraging heartfelt words, but who do people say I am? What do others really see when they see me? Before getting to know me, what do they see? The phone almost immediately beeped with the question **"Do you want us to be honest?"** I became a little worried but texted back immediately, "Yes!" I became worried not because I knew what they would say, but because I always go out of my way to not hurt others' feelings. I try to show the love of Christ because as a representative of who He is, I try to represent him well. I encourage others when I need encouraging myself, I give to others even when I don't have it to give. I do not boast about what I do. I never dishearten others. What could they possibly have to say? As my mind continued to run all over the place, the phone beeped. I took a deep breath and began to read the incoming text. The first text said "Sometimes, jealousy concerning your husband," "Mean when you do not smile," (two people liked this comment) and someone had even called me "Biggity". These comments made me feel some kind of way, but I kept reading because it is a blessing to have people around you who are willing to tell you the truth and not what you want to hear. It is people who love you enough to tell you the truth that will push you into growth. Now that my feelings are kind of hurt, these comments force me to take a deeper look at myself to understand why someone would attach these words to my name. So now the real work begins.

As we begin this journey, I ask that we be honest with ourselves. This is our personal healing place, and there is no one here to impress. There is only one expectation, and that is for us to be honest with ourselves and be free from the bondage of what other people think and expect.

Keeping this in mind, I began my journey and I asked myself the questions again, but this time looking in the mirror. I asked the question, "WHO ARE YOU? When you are not being what others need and expect you to be, who are you?" And as I looked in the mirror (not just a glimpse) but to stare in the eyes of the person looking back at me, tears began to fall because I realized I did not truly know the person that was there, because the person I described is who everyone expects me to be. But if I am truly honest with myself, these things are only half of who I am. The part of me that people do not know and never get to see is a scared, self-conscious woman trapped in a little girl's mindset, who battles depression and was violated by a family friend, and due to fear and embarrassment, she was forced to grow up because time never stopped and gave her the opportunity to heal. (Wow.) Being truly honest caused me to realize I have been living a lie most of my life. I have been living a life that satisfied who people and society think I should be and never took the time to embrace who I really am.

I have lived a life of a BEAUTIFUL BONDAGE. A life pleasing to the senses but enslaved to my past.

Does this sound familiar?

Now take the time to examine your life and try it again.

Who Are You?

On the lines below, answer the question, who are you?

If you cannot think of full sentences, just list a cluster of words of past experiences that may have had an impact on the way you see life.

_____

_____

_____

_____

_____

_____

_____

_____

_____

_____

_____

_____

_____

_____

_____

_____

_____

**We have been through every emotion, but now we have come to a place of awareness, and this is where we need to be so we can now begin to heal.**

In the last few days, what problems in your life have you discovered need to be addressed?

PROBLEM LIST

★ _____

★ _____

★ _____

★ _____

Now look in the mirror (a full-length mirror is preferred). I know your first instinct is to fix what you consider to be wrong, whether it be your hair, eyebrows, or clothing. This activity requires you to not fix anything; just look at yourself and ask the person in the mirror WHO ARE YOU? Now write down the first things that come to mind. Remember these are your private thoughts and be honest.

_____

_____

_____

_____

_____

_____

_____

_____

_____

_____

_____

_____

_____

**Who do people say you are?**

On the lines below, fill in what people see when they see you. (It is okay to ask others to help with this portion because how we think people perceive us, is not always the truth.) You may be surprised (like I was) at their answers.

_____

_____

_____

_____

_____

_____

_____

_____

_____

_____

_____

_____

_____

_____

_____

_____

_____

_____

It is very important to understand that the truth is what makes us better. Although sometimes hearing the truth is hard, it will or should force us to identify areas that can use work in our lives. These activities are designed to empower, encourage, and motivate each of us to be the best we can be. Take a few moments to receive what has been said and try to identify what area of your life pushed you to this behavior. We are beautiful, loved, and sometimes misunderstood, and maybe this is because we truly do not understand ourselves. After all, we are all just trying to make it. Our feelings may be hurt at this point to know how people really experience us but focus on this: **THE TRUTH WILL SET YOU FREE.** If we never face the truth, then we will never truly be free.

Yesterday, we took a few moments to receive what was said about us; we had to identify what area or areas of our lives pushed us to this type of behavior.

So today, we will list an event or events that we have experienced publicly or privately that we feel have deeply impacted our lives (remember to be honest). It is the truth that will set you free. We are all entitled to our feelings. These things are at the core of why we do what we do.

| Positive | Negative |
|---|---|
|  |  |
|  |  |
|  |  |
|  |  |
|  |  |
|  |  |

I know this activity may have been a little harder than it seems. Being asked to write the positive, after becoming aware of the negative, is somewhat hard to do. This yet again is an activity we can implement into our day-to-day lives. When life gives us hard unwanted encounters, we can acknowledge them, be aware that it has happened, but find ways to deal with the problem at hand in a healthy manner. One way of doing this is by NOT living in **Beautifully Organized Bondage** (tucking the situation away and acting as if it never happened). For years, I lived with this strategy, and I will be the first to say, **IT DOES NOT WORK!** The hide, protect, and pretend mindset will have you living a roller-coaster of a life. **Surrounded by people but still feeling alone, suicidal, and depressed, struggling every day to get out of bed just to pretend like everything is okay. Waking up every morning trying your best, to be for others what NO ONE could be for you.** Until we heal by facing our situations head on, we can only pretend to be happy. The season of pretending is over. God cannot heal what we are not willing to face.

Now look in the mirror and fill in the blanks.

(Use some of your negatives from above)

_____ happened to me and because of it I feel _____.

The Projected Path to a Better You

List the habits that are damaging.

_____

_____

_____

_____

_____

_____

_____

_____

Taking him by the right hand, he helped him up, and instantly the man's feet and ankles became strong. He jumped to his feet and began to walk. Then he went with them into the temple courts, walking and jumping, and praising God. **Acts 3:7-8**

Sometimes our lives can look like this man's story. Because we have been in a situation for so long, it sometimes can appear that we are receiving what we need to survive. We are so blinded by pain, circumstances, brokenness, deception, and hurt that we become adjusted to and comfortable in beautiful bondage. We become comfortable in bondage because sometimes it's all we know. Therefore, leaving us like this man in survival living rather than living in and on purpose. Take this time to reflect on the things that has been discovered in the past few days.

Now that we have come face-to-face with our uncomfortable reality, the true work begins. Our foundations are where we began, and no matter how bad the foundations were, we must grow from what we were giving. The good thing is we can use what we have as an encouragement to do better, or we can allow our foundations to hinder, rob, and/or distort our future. During this journey, we will use the Bible as a guiding light to recognize and embrace our true selves. We use the Bible as our guide because it is always wise to read and use the instructions from the manufacturer of a thing. It is the manufacturer who knows why the object was created and the correct function of the thing. It would not be wise to read our car manual to learn how to operate our television. So, it is not wise to look to the views of this world for direction and instruction on how we should operate. Our journey has already begun, but the remainder of this journey will teach us to see ourselves how God sees us and not as the world sees us nor what our circumstances tell us we must be. In the clouds below, jot down a few things you have discovered in just seven days that could be clouding your view of the real you.

Reward yourself! You deserve it!

Foundation Problems

"Before I formed you in the womb I knew you, before you were born, I set you apart; I appointed you as a prophet to the nations". **Jeremiah 1:5**

Today's journey begins by reminding us that just like Jeremiah, God thought about us and knew us before we were born. Sometimes it is very easy to lose sight of this truth. So often we look to the family in which we were born as a foundation of what we are and what we can become. This concept in some cases limits us from the very beginning. For example, some people are the product of one-night stands, rapes, adoption, incest, left by a parent who never returned or were even born into poverty. It is very important that we focus on **who** rather than how. Our parents were only used as a vehicle to get us here, but what is in us is more important than the labels of our families that are on us. Each of us was called before we were born. This means that each of us has a worth. We have a value far beyond our earthly family tree. When we follow that pattern of the "how" instead of the "who," we will look at who our earthly family is and begin to believe the worldly hype. For example, you are just like your daddy, while your daddy on earth has never discovered himself and showed up on earth as a third-generation alcoholic.

Today is the first day of the rest of your life. It is time to change what you see and believe about yourself. When you feel discouraged, or inadequate, remember that God has always thought of you as valuable. Yes, God thought about you and made plans for you before you were even conceived. Not only did he think about you, but he planned for you, He loves you and He created you for a purpose. Are there some things from your foundations (past/childhood) that negatively affected your life?

_____

_____

_____

_____

_____

_____

_____

_____

_____

_____

It's okay to have a few cracks in the foundation because I can assure you that you are not the only one. Some of us just hide ours well. The good news is we won't leave them there to get worse.

If you could make a wish and when you woke up this morning everything was perfect, what would your life look like? Ask yourself this question: What would my best self-look like?

In this activity, we are prompted to imagine and write about our best possible selves in three areas. Throughout the next few days, our responses will be used to guide a daily visualization practice. Immediately after the writing portion of the exercise, take time to practice visualization.

### <u>Seeing a Better Me!</u>

*What you see is ultimately what you will be*

*So, let's work on seeing*

### Writing

- We will imagine and describe our best possible self in three areas: personal, professional, and social.

### Visualize

- For the next several days, we should spend **five minutes** each day visualizing our best possible self. We should focus on one area per day throughout the week.

### How to perform visualization exercise.

**Picture your best possible self in as many details as possible. Think of scenes (places) that you might find yourself in and imagine sights, sounds, and feelings you would experience.**

**Write or draw what that place or situation would look, feel, sound like to you.**

**Personal Domain**

**Things that fall under our personal domain: skills, hobbies, health, accomplishments, etc.**

---

**"Humble yourself before the Lord, and He will lift you up in honor." James 4:10**

---

We must always recognize that our worth comes from God alone. To be humble, we must lean on his power and guidance and not go our own independent way. Although we do not deserve God's favor, He wants to lift us up and give us worth and dignity, despite our human shortcomings. God does not have to make us into something he created us to be we must take back our identity that was stripped away by the sins of this world.

**Step 1:** Imagine your best possible self in the **personal** domain for one minute

**Step 2:** Now write about your best self in the **personal** domain for five minutes. Continue writing for the entire time, using as much detail as possible.

_____

_____

_____

_____

_____

**Great job!**

**For I know the plans I have for you," declares the Lord, "plans to prosper you and not to harm you, plans to give you hope and a future. Jeremiah 29:11**

God knows the future, and his plans for us are good and full of hope. Now please do not receive this as meaning that we will not have pain, suffering, and hardship. Those things are a sure part of life in this sinful world. What this does mean is that God will see us through.

**Step 1:** Imagine the best possible self in the **Personal** domain for one minute

**Step 2:** Now write about your best self in the **Personal** domain for five minutes. Continue writing for the entire time, using as much detail as possible.

_____

_____

_____

_____

_____

_____

_____

_____

Way to go!

## Professional Domain

**Things that fall under the professional domain: job, sense of purpose, education, skills, retirement, income, etc.**

❧

**All hard work brings a profit, but mere talk leads only to poverty. Proverbs 14:23**

❧

Plain and simple, don't talk about it, be about it. Talking does not get the job done, but hard work will pay off. Talking does not get the business started, doing the work does. Sometimes it may take a little longer than expected, but keep working; eventually, it will happen.

**Step 1:** Imagine the best possible self in the **Professional** domain for one minute

**Step 2:** Now write about your best self in the **Professional** domain for five minutes. Continue writing for the entire time, using as much detail as possible.

_____

_____

_____

_____

_____

_____

_____

_____

**You did great!**

**May the favor of the Lord our God rest on us; establish the work of our hands for us—yes, establish the work of our hands. Psalm 90:17**

It is a desire for most of us that the work we do is counted, acknowledged, and appreciated. We all wish to be effective and productive in the work that we do. But the truth is our work will not always be acknowledged, it will not always be appreciated, but we must not allow that to stop us from doing the work. Sometimes we must encourage ourselves knowing that one day, we will receive the reward we deserve for the work we have done.

**Step 1:** Imagine the best possible self in the **Professional** domain for one minute

**Step 2:** Now write about your best self in the **Professional** domain for five minutes. Continue writing for the entire time, using as much detail as possible.

_____

_____

_____

_____

_____

_____

_____

_____

_____

**You can do this!**

## Social Domain

**Things that fall under Social Domain: romantic relationship, friends, family, social activities, etc.**

---

**"Therefore, as we have the opportunity, let us do good to all people, especially to those who belong to the family of believers." Galatians 6:10**

---

It can be discouraging to continue to do right and receive no word of thanks or see no tangible results. But Paul challenged the Galatians, and he challenges us to keep on doing good and to trust God for the results. Be encouraged that in due time, we will reap a harvest of blessings.

**Step 1:** Imagine the best possible self in the **Social** domain for one minute

**Step 2:** Now write about your best self in the **Social** domain for five minutes. Continue writing for the entire time, using as much detail as possible.

_____

_____

_____

_____

_____

_____

_____

**You did it!**

**So, in everything, do to others what you would have them do to you, for this sums up the Law and the Prophets. Matthew 7:12**

Sometimes it can be a challenge to take the initiative in doing something good for some people. But here Jesus formulated it in a way that demonstrates a foundation of active goodness and mercy. This is the same kind of love God shows to us every day. So today, think of a good and merciful action you can take today.

**Step 1:** Imagine the best possible self in the **Social** domain for one minute

**Step 2:** Now write about your best self in the **Social** domain for five minutes. Continue writing for the entire time, using as much detail as possible.

_____

_____

_____

_____

_____

_____

_____

_____

_____

Great Job!

**Do not conform to the pattern of this world but be transformed by the renewing of your mind. Then you will be able to test and approve what God's will is—his good, pleasing, and perfect will. Romans 12:2**

We must constantly be on the lookout for the worldly system versus God's system. Worldly systems will always try to conform us to its ungodly patterns. Just because we come from a particular neighborhood does not mean we cannot rise above it. Just because you have past indiscretions does not mean your life is over, and you must look like what you have been through. We must see ourselves as better. A very important piece to a better life is winning the battles that begin in our minds.

Congratulations! You are doing great.

**Step 1:** Imagine the best possible self in the **Personal, Professional, and Social** domain for one to two minutes.

**Step 2:** Now write about your best self in the **Personal, Professional, and Social** domain for five minutes. Continue writing for the entire time, using as much detail as possible.

_____

_____

_____

_____

_____

_____

**Congratulations! You made it!**

The Projected Path to a Better You

List how you will monitor bad habits and attitudes, but also lists ways to replace the bad habits and attitudes.

_____

_____

_____

_____

_____

_____

_____

_____

The problem is not what happens to me, the problem is how I respond to what happened to me! (Read it again.)

WOW!

We are aware of what is; for the last few pages we have imagined what could be.

Now, what are some ways that can be used to improve your life for the better?

**Solution List**

★ _____

★ _____

★ _____

★ _____

**Do something special for yourself! You deserve it!**

WHY WE DO WHAT WE DO?

Our core beliefs are our most central ideas about ourselves, others, and the world. These beliefs act like a lens through which every situation and life experience is seen. Because of this, people with different core beliefs might be in the same situation, but think, feel, and act differently. Two can have experienced the same hurt but handle it in two different ways. The next few days we will simplify the definition of core beliefs, along with examples showing how they affect thoughts, behaviors, and our feelings. After examining how our core beliefs can affect our lives, we will then identify how they have affected our lives. Then we will set in place plans to overcome the things that once held us bound! HINT: notice I said ONCE, prepare yourself for the mind shift that is getting ready to happen.

Even if a core belief is inaccurate, it still shapes how we see the world around us. Harmful core beliefs lead to negative thoughts, feelings, and behaviors, whereas rational core beliefs lead to balanced reactions.

**Sample Situation**: Two people with different core beliefs receive a bad grade on a test.

Person A may have the response "I am a failure." Their thought is, of course, I failed . . . why bother? These people may also deal with behaviors of depression and make no effort to change the situation.

Whereas Person B has a different response. Person B's response is "I am perfectly capable of passing the test when I give my best effort." This person's thoughts are, "I did poorly because I did not prepare for the test." Instead of feeling depressed, this person feels disappointed and makes plans to study before the next test.

Common Harmful Core Beliefs: Core beliefs are often hidden beneath surface-level beliefs. For example, the core belief "no one likes me" might underlie the surface belief "my friends only spend time with me out of pity". This person may feel helpless, therefore believing they are weak, a loser, trapped, unlovable, and that they will end up alone. They may feel that no one likes them, they are worthless, bad people, and sometimes believe that they do not deserve to live. Harmful core beliefs have one always on guard for external danger. They feel that the world is a dangerous place and people cannot be trusted. They feel like nothing ever goes right for them. The consequences of harmful core beliefs are interpersonal problems such as difficulty trusting others, feelings of inadequacy in relationships, excessive jealousy, overly confrontational or aggressive behavior, and putting others' needs above one's own needs. Harmful core beliefs also affect our mental health and cause us to suffer from problems of depression, anxiety, substance abuse, difficulty handling stress, and low self-esteem. Here are a few facts about core beliefs:

- People are not born with core beliefs—they are learned.
- Core beliefs usually develop in childhood, or during stressful or traumatic periods in adulthood.
- Information that contradicts core beliefs is often ignored.
- Negative core beliefs are not necessarily true, even if they feel true.
- Core beliefs tend to be rigid and long-standing. However, they can be changed.

So why we do what we do is because of what we believe.

Now that we are more familiar with negative core beliefs, what are some negative core beliefs you have? I will go first.

\* <u>I am not smart enough</u>
\* <u>I am unworthy of good things</u>
\* <u>The world is a dangerous place, and people cannot be trusted.</u>

Now it's your turn, and remember, honesty is the key that unlocks our peace.

## THE TRUTH WILL SET YOU FREE!!

★ _____

★ _____

★ _____

★ _____

Please understand that everyone is entitled to their feelings.

We never realize how much our past has controlled our present in both positive and negative ways. There are things that we have never attempted to go after; we counted ourselves out, we did not feel it was within our reach because we did not feel worthy. Look in your mirror and say these words to the person looking back.

Finish the sentence below.

YOU ARE DESERVING OF _____

YOU ARE WORTHY OF _____

YOU CAN HAVE _____

Say it until the one who is looking back believes it. Throughout this day, be reminded by announcing it into the atmosphere. This time making it personal.

I am deserving of _____

I am worthy of _____

I can have _____

Now believe it!

Congratulations!

Today we will put our thoughts on trial. We will act as an attorney, prosecutor, and judge, as we compare evidence for and against a single thought. Like in a real court of law, only verifiable facts are admissible as evidence. Opinions, assumptions, and conjectures are not allowed. Let's explore.

What is a negative thought you have?

_____

_____

_____

_____

_____

_____

Defense: What REAL evidence do you have for this thought?

_____

_____

_____

_____

_____

_____

Then Jesus said, "Did I not tell you that if you **believe**, you will **see** the glory of God?"

When I was a child, I would often hear the older members of my family say, "I have to see that to believe it." Therefore, I grew up with the same mindset. A prime example of being blinded to the things that will one day impact our lives because of what we believe. A lot of things in life, I did not attempt to do because I had no evidence of it happening for people like me. A lot of things I believe could not happen for me because of hurt people hurting me or people who I thought loved me and had my best interest at heart gave compelling evidence why I could not do it.

The outcome of believing the hurt was years of misery and silent pain. Jesus said if you believe, you will see the glory of God. It has taken me thirty-five years and a school called the Hope Bible Institute to shift and develop awareness of my identity. This school forced me to believe what the WORD OF GOD said concerning me and not the world.

On the lines below list as much evidence as possible to prove why your negative thoughts are not true.

_____

_____

_____

_____

_____

Because of the importance of self-gratification, we will put our thoughts on trial again today.

What is a negative thought you have or have had in the past few days?

_____

_____

_____

_____

Defense: What REAL evidence do you have for this thought?

_____

_____

_____

_____

_____

Prosecutor: Now what evidence do you have against this thought? Gather and present on the lines below as much evidence as possible to prove why this negative thought is not true.

_____

_____

_____

_____

_____

_____

If you notice, there are not as many lines to prove against our negative thoughts. This is because often we have, or should I say believe to have, more evidence of why we should not receive the good things. So, if you could only think of one proof why the negative is not real, you are doing great. This is a shift we must adjust to and that is okay but remind yourself repeatedly of the positive and not the negative.

I am deserving of _____

I am worthy of _____

I can have _____

Congratulations! You did it again!

Prosecutor: Now what evidence do you have against this thought? Gather and present on the lines below.

_____

_____

_____

_____

_____

_____

If you notice, this time our lines have increased for the positive feedback. This is because we have been practicing the shift of thinking by searching within ourselves for better evidence of why we should receive good things.

I am deserving of _____

I am worthy of _____

I can have _____

Congratulations! You did it again!

Romans 8:28

And we know that all things work together for good to them that love God, to them who are called according to his purpose.

It is very important that we understand that God works in everything. He does not work in just the good things but all things. Although all things that happen to us are not pleasant, and we do not have to call them good. God can take every circumstance and use it for our long-term good. Yes, the hurtful, heartbreaking, paralyzing things that have happened to us, God can use them for good. This promise is for those who love God and are called according to his purpose. Such people have new perspectives and a new mindset.

For the next few activities, we will be focusing on gratitude rather than negative.

1.  Name at least one good thing you expect to happen today.

_____

_____

_____

_____

2. What were some good things you saw someone do for you or someone else?

_____

_____

_____

_____

3. Today you smiled when . . .

_____

_____

_____

_____

Congratulations! You found and focused on the good rather than bad!!!

Rejoice always, pray continually, give thanks in all circumstances; for this is God's will for you in Christ Jesus. 1 Thessalonians 5:16–18

When we make a conscious decision to do what God says, we will begin to see people, things, and the situation in a new perspective, and we will have an easier time being joyful. Evil does not come from God, so we should not thank him for it. But when evil strikes, we can still be thankful for God's presence and the good he will accomplish in and through the distress. For example, God is now using the hurt and pain of my past to empower you. He is now using what I thought was dirty and no good as a beacon of light to motivate other people to trust Him.

We tend to focus on our negative experiences far more than our positive experiences. Think about it. If you receive a negative evaluation at work, or you miss an important question on a test, it sticks out like a sore thumb. It does not matter if 95 percent of the feedback you receive is positive—the negative 5 percent is what you are going to think about. This is true in just about every aspect of life. A single fight with a friend will feel so much bigger than the hundreds of positive interactions that came before it.

A gratitude journal will force you to put positive and negative experiences into perspective. Instead of ending each day with thoughts of what went wrong, you'll spend a few minutes thinking about what went right. Instead of waking up and focusing on what went wrong yesterday, this activity will motivate you to be grateful and focus on the positive. Additionally, a gratitude journal will get you in the habit of noticing positive experiences as they happen and giving them more attention.

What are some things you can be proud of?

_____

_____

_____

List some experiences you feel lucky to have had:

_____

_____

_____

What is an unexpected, good thing that has happened to you?

_____

_____

_____

All this is for your benefit, so that the grace that is reaching more and more people may cause thanksgiving to overflow to the glory of God. 2 Corinthians 4:15

In this life, we all must face suffering, distress, and trials. But we must constantly remind ourselves that they will one day be over. As we face great troubles, it is easy to focus on our pain rather than the ultimate good that will come of it. Just as when an athlete focuses on the finish line, they ignore the discomfort, we too must focus on the reward of our faith and the joy that will last forever.

Did you know that our persistence in prayer expresses our faith that God answers prayer? So, when you feel tired of praying, remember that God sees you, knows what you need, always listens, and wants to do great work through you. God may not always answer in the ways we expect, but He will always answer in the way He knows is best for us. DON'T STOP BELIEVING!

How has another person shown that they care about you within the past week?

_____

_____

_____

What is something nice you said in the past week?

_____

_____

_____

Describe a personal strength you used today:

_____

_____

_____

Cast all your anxieties on him, because he cares for you. Be sober-minded; be watchful. Your adversary the devil prowls around like a roaring lion, seeking someone to devour. Resist him, firm in your faith, knowing that the same kinds of suffering are being experienced by your brotherhood throughout the world. 1 Peter 5:7–9

Lions attack sick, young, and straggling animals; they choose victims who are alone or not alert. We must watch out for the ways of the enemy when we are suffering or being persecuted. When you are feeling alone, helpless, and cutoff from others, or when you are so focused on troubles that you forget to watch for danger, you are vulnerable to Satan's attack.

But carrying our worries, stress, and daily struggles to God is a clear indication that we find assurance in letting Him carry our burdens. This says I have no confidence in the circumstance, but I do have confidence in God, the one who controls the circumstance.

I know that life has brought some struggles, joys, and pain but God will use all of it for your good.

By filling in the blanks below, we will create love notes to ourselves.

**To:**

**Thank you for being my** _____
**I appreciate you because . . .**

1. _____

2. _____

3. _____

**I think you are special because you make me laugh when**

_____

_____

_____

**I have fun with you when**

_____

_____

_____

**You are important to me because**

_____

_____

_____

**When I think about you, I feel**

_____

_____

_____

**From: Date:**

You did it!

———————————————— ❧ ————————————————

**There is therefore now no condemnation to them who are in Christ Jesus, who walk not after the flesh but after the Spirit. Romans 8:1**

———————————————— ❧ ————————————————

The word "condemnation" means that there is an expression of very strong disapproval and censure. It means the action of condemning someone to a punishment, a sentencing.

NOT GUILTY. LET THE PERSON GO FREE. What would those words mean to you if you were on death row? In reality, the whole world should be on death row. But thank God, He has declared us NOT GUILTY and has offered us freedom from sin. I want you to take a few moments to process what you just read. YOU ARE NOT GUILTY! YOU ARE FREE TO GO! Free from what, you may ask. You are FREE TO GO from past pain, disappointment, and mistakes. YOU ARE FREE TO WALK AWAY FROM IT ALL.

Yes, you did it, and yes, they did hurt you. But don't let your past hold your future hostage any longer. Today you meet the you that you have never seen before.

The words I AM are powerful. "I am" says something about you that no one can take away. For the next six days, you will make a declaration about your life. Each day, the affirmations will increase. (Look in the mirror, speak boldly until the person looking back believes it.)

# DAY ONE

I AM FREE FOREVER FROM CONDEMNATION

I AM ASSURED THAT ALL THINGS WORK TOGETHER FOR MY GOOD

I AM FREE FROM ALL CONDEMNING CHARGES AGAINST ME

I AM BLESSED

I AM VALUABLE

I AM FEARFULLY AND WONDERFULLY MADE

I AM BECOMING ALL GOD CREATED ME TO BE

I HAVE BEEN ESTABLISHED, ANOINTED, AND SEALED BY GOD

I AM _____

I AM _____

You should be proud of yourself!

# Day Two

Philippians 1:6

God is the one who **began** this **good work in you**, and I am certain that **He** won't stop before it is complete on the day that Christ Jesus returns.

"The work of grace has its root in the divine goodness of the Father, it is planted by the self-denying goodness of the Son, and it is daily watered by the goodness of the Holy Spirit; it springs from good and leads to good, and so is altogether good. Because this good work was begun, Paul was confident, and every believer should be confident of its completion. God is a worker who completes His works. If only you would believe.

This time, as you say you're I AM, I want you to say it out loud like you believe it. WHY, because you are too good of a work for God to give up on you. You are too good of a work for God to forget about you and leave you for dead. But YOU have to believe.

I AM THAT I AM

I AM FREE FOREVER FROM CONDEMNATION

I AM ASSURED THAT ALL THINGS WORK TOGETHER FOR MY GOOD

I AM FREE FROM ALL CONDEMNING CHARGES AGAINST ME

I AM BLESSED

I AM VALUABLE

I AM FEARFULLY AND WONDERFULLY MADE

I AM BECOMING ALL GOD CREATED ME TO BE

## I HAVE BEEN ESTABLISHED, ANOINTED, AND SEALED BY GOD

I AM _____

I AM _____

I AM _____

I AM _____

You should be proud of yourself!

# DAY THREE

Welcome to the courtroom of your mind/life:

---
ᘇᘻᘖ
---

Let God be true, and every human being is a liar. As it is written: "So that you may be proved right when you speak and prevail when you judge." Romans 3:4

---
ᘖᘻᘇ
---

Below, we will practice defending our future from false accusations and evidence presented by the world and our past mistakes. REMEMBER, YOU ARE NOT GUILTY! Let nothing and no one hold you captive because of the old you. Old things have passed away. Behold, all things have become new.

Old Mindset verses New Mindset

**Example**: **I AM NOT** A lost cause      (something someone has called you)

**Because I AM** ESTABLISHED, ANOINTED, AND SEALED BY GOD

Your turn (if you can't do all three spaces, that's fine, but try to do at least one).

**I AM NOT** _____
**Because I AM** _____

**I AM NOT** _____
**Because I AM** _____

**I AM NOT** _____
**Because I AM** _____

43

# DAY FOUR

❧❧

Therefore, if anyone is in Christ, the new creation has come: The old has gone, the new is here! **2 Corinthians 5:17**

❧❧

The resurrection of Jesus gives us new life. This is a promise for anyone. It doesn't matter what class, what race, what nationality, what language, or what level of intelligence. Anyone can be a new creation in Jesus Christ. So, we are told to put off the old man (old you) and put on the new man (new you) which was created according to God, in righteousness and true holiness. All things that have become new is the language of God's perfect, recreated work. God wants to do a new thing in your life. You are responsible for fighting for your future. Take court seriously this time by believing what you write and then look in the mirror and speak over your life.

**I AM NOT** _____
**Because I AM** _____

**I AM NOT** _____
**Because I AM** _____

**I AM NOT** _____
**Because I AM** _____

**I AM NOT** _____
**Because I AM** _____

**I AM NOT** _____
**Because I AM** _____

**I am so proud of you!**
**Treat yourself today**

# DAY FIVE

Truly, I say to you, whoever says to this mountain, "Be taken up and thrown into the sea," and does not doubt in his heart, but believes that what he says will come to pass, it will be done for him. **Mark 11:23**

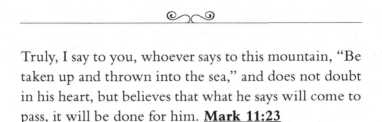

There is nothing you have ever been through that God cannot break you free from. To change a situation, we must first change the way we see things. For example, I survived sexual abuse, but I didn't see it as survival, I saw myself as a victim. So, I lived as a victim. This mindset affected everything I did, how I lived, and how I loved. But once I truly understood that the thing that hurt me was not a representation of who I was, my life began to change. So today, continue to remove the mountains of your past that are holding you hostage today. Your past is not who you are, it is just a part of your story. You are not a victim, you, my friend, are a victor because you survived. You my friend are a person who has defeated an enemy in battle.

**Today, start your very own I AM declarations.**

**I AM** _____

**I AM** _____

**I AM** _____

**I AM** _____

**I AM** _____

## WRITE THEM AGAIN IN A DIFFERENT COLOR

I AM _____

I AM _____

I AM _____

I AM _____

I AM _____

**Celebrate yourself!**

# DAY SIX

❦

Death and life are in the power of the tongue, and those who love it will eat its fruits. **Proverbs 18:21**

❦

Here the idea is extended to remind us that the tongue not only has the power of provision but also of death and life. Those who are wise enough to love and appreciate the power of what a man says will be blessed and will eat the pleasant fruit of wise and effective speech. So many times, we have spoken death (negative) over our careers, relationships, and life in general. We speak these things (your/I'm just like your/my daddy) then we are upset when the fruit of what we say shows up. Today continue to Speak LIFE (POSITIVE) things over your life.

**You/I said** _____

**It's not true because GOD said** _____

**I AM** _____

You/I said _____

It's not true because GOD said _____

I AM _____

**You/I said** _____

**It's not true because GOD said** _____

**I AM** _____

You/I said _____

It's not true because GOD said _____

I AM _____

**You/I said** _____

**It's not true because GOD said** _____

**I AM** _____

# Day Seven

## 1 Peter 2:24

He himself bore our sins in his body on the tree, that we might die to sin and live to righteousness. By his wounds, you have been healed.

The suffering of Jesus is an example for us, but it is far more than an example. He also bore our sins as a sin-bearing substitute and provided for our healing. Our life is permanently changed by our identification with Jesus on the cross. We have died to sin in the sense that our debt of sin and guilt was paid by Jesus's sacrifice on the cross. When we died to sin with Jesus on the cross, it means that He paid our debts. We do not trouble ourselves over debts that are paid. "He who bore my sins in His own body on the tree, took all my debts and paid them for me, and now I am dead to those debts; they have no power over me. I am dead to my sins; Christ suffered instead of me. I have nothing to do with them. They are gone as much as if they had never been committed." NOT GUILTY, YOU ARE FREE TO GO! Did you know that we can sometimes spend our entire life trying to pay for a single mistake? Today is the day you forgive yourself. Forgiving ourselves can sometimes be challenging but knowing that the debt has already been paid can make the process easier. Don't hold yourself hostage to a thing that Jesus has died to free you from.

Say your I AM with confidence today.

I AM _____

I AM _____

I AM _____

I AM _____

I AM _____

**I AM** _____

**I AM** _____

**I AM** _____

**I AM** _____

**I AM** _____

My prayer is that you now have begun to believe what you are saying.

Celebrate your progress!

The Projected Path to a Better You

List how you will NO LONGER MONITOR bad habits and attitudes, but NOW LIST STEPS OR WAYS YOU WILL ACTIVELY CHANGE OR REPLACE bad habits and attitudes.

_____

_____

_____

_____

_____

_____

Patience is good, but understanding is so much better. Patience runs out, but understanding delivers compassion, and compassion causes one to do something about the situation.

That same love, support, and companionship we lend to others must also be administered in our own lives. It's called self-care. In your list below, what steps of self-care will you take to help replace old habits and thoughts?

**Solution List**

★ _____

★ _____

★ _____

★ _____

**Do something special for yourself! You deserve it!**

Love thy neighbor as thyself, I can't properly love you if I don't love me.

For the past few days we have been writing I AM affirmations for our life. The words "I am" are so powerful in our lives because the I AM we believe is what ultimately shows up in our day to day lives. What you see and believe about your past, present, and future is what you will be.

So now here we are, deep in this journey, and we ask the question again:

WHO AM I?

_____

_____

_____

_____

_____

_____

_____

_____

_____

_____

If we change our minds, we change our life.

In the spaces below, write a letter to yourself. I will share a few lines of my letter.

**<u>Dear Linda</u>**

**<u>Hey girl, it is so nice to finally meet you. For a long time, I never knew you existed. If I am honest, I wanted to stop searching for you before I ever began because I feared you were not real. But now that I have connected with you, I vow to never lose sight of you again. I will fight every day for your peace, your joy, and your success. I will never lose you again trying to be what others want you to be. I will do the necessary work that you will walk in victory, and not despair. You are worth love and respect. You are worthy of good things. Girl, you are beautiful, smart, powerful, and a world changer. You are worth fighting for. I promise to never give up on you, and . . . . . . . .</u>**

NOW IT'S YOUR TURN

## TAKE YOUR POWER BACK

_____

_____

_____

_____

_____

_____

_____

_____

_____

_____

_____

_____

_____

_____

_____

_____

_____

_____

With Love

_____

NOW IT'S TIME YOU LIVE AND NOT JUST EXIST
LOOKING FORWARD TO HEARING YOUR TESTIMONY

Printed in the United States
by Baker & Taylor Publisher Services